AVA SPARK
Hello, I'm Here!

For Jessica, Luke, Helena, James and Grace
Forever Five – **A F**
For Spencer, Eva and Hamish xxx – **J B**

First published in Great Britain 2025
by New Frontier Publishing Europe Ltd
Vicarage House, 58-60 Kensington Church Street, London W8 4DB
www.newfrontierpublishing.co.uk

978-1-916790-55-1 (PB) • 978-1-916790-58-2 (eBook)

Text © 2025 Alex Field
Illustrations © 2025 Joanna Bartel
All rights reserved.

The rights of the author and illustrator have been asserted.

This book is sold subject to the condition that it shall not, by way of trade
or otherwise, be lent, hired out or otherwise circulated in any form of binding
or cover other than that in which it is published. No part of this publication may be
reproduced, stored in a retrieval system, or transmitted, in any form or by any means
(electronic, mechanical, photocopying, recording or otherwise), without the
prior written permission of New Frontier Publishing Europe Ltd.

A CIP catalogue record for this book is available from the British Library.

Edited by Tasha Evans • Designed by Verity Clark and Jenny Stephenson

Printed in China
1 3 5 7 9 10 8 6 4 2

#sparkaconversation

AVA SPARK
Hello, I'm Here!

NEW FRONTIER PUBLISHING

Name: Ava Spark – It's disappointing, I know. I wish I had a more glamorous name.

Age: 10 years, 1 month and 2 days

Lives with: Mum and my twin sister, Flo, short for Florence

School: Little Park Primary School

Best friends: Jack and Miya

When I grow up, I want to be: A chef or maybe a baker – we eat a lot of cake in my house.

I CAN HEAR YOU

'**AAARE YOUUU LISTENING?**' Mrs Hare says slowly and loudly to me.

Mrs Hare is our new teacher, and she's definitely not **COOL**. She wears shoes with Velcro, and she's an **ADULT**.

Jack says, 'She can hear you!' to Mrs Hare, and everyone in the class is silent.

Mrs Hare's face turns **bright** red, and I think she might **explode**.

Jack speaks as if absolutely nothing scary has just happened. 'Ava talks using her machine. She was writing something. I'll show you.' Mrs Hare stands behind me and looks at my machine. I had started writing **DEN** but deleted it when Mrs Hare started shouting.

'Ava looks at the alphabet on her machine with her eyes, and then it writes the words. It's a communication aid, and it's how Ava

talks, using her eyes,' Jack says importantly.

Mrs Hare looks **confused**.

'When Ava has written all her words, she looks at the speech button, and it speaks her words out loud. She can even save phrases for later. It's really **cool**.'

Mrs Hare frowns, her forehead wrinkling, but she nods her head and says, 'I see.'

Jack is my best friend in the whole world. On day one of primary school, my mum accidentally ran over his foot with my wheelchair. Luckily, I said, **'Sorry,'** and he said, 'That's okay,' and we have been **best friends** ever since.

When the bell rings, Jack pushes me in my wheelchair. He parks me in our **DEN**, under a tree in the shade. It's our **not-so-secret** meeting place.

Jack can be quite serious. He's always super careful when wheeling me about the place. Sometimes I say to him, 'Let's go **fast**.' He never thinks it's a good idea.

Miya (she's also my friend) and Jack have known each other longer than me and Jack. They were babies together and they live next door to each other.

Their mums are **mad** runners. By mad, I mean they run for miles and miles. They are training for the London Marathon, which is a really long race that takes four hours – sometimes even longer.

Jack is not at all like his mum. He runs nowhere.

Jack's mum is forever trying to get him to go **outside**.

'Why don't you go and ride your bike with Miya?' she says. Jack never rides his bike with Miya. One time Jack was pushing me home and Miya flew past us with her legs hanging down either side of her bike. She was screaming at the top of her lungs as she raced down the hill.

'She's going to fall off,' Jack said, looking worried. I think it all looks like **brilliant** fun.

Miya arrived late to school today, again. Her mum forgot to set her alarm. This happens quite often.

I think it might be to do with all the running. Maybe her mum needs **extra** sleep to keep running. Anyway, Miya missed our first lesson with the dreaded Mrs Hare.

We have been talking for days about Mrs Hare. We have seen her walking the corridors.

We always know when Mrs Hare is coming down the corridor. You can hear her **squelching** in her funny shoes.

Miya stands up and walks like Mrs Hare, making **squelching** noises with her mouth. She sticks her bottom out just like Mrs Hare does too. Even Jack laughs. This is a **MIRACLE**. He doesn't laugh very often.

Miya asks me if she is as horrible as we thought she might be. There have been rumours. I look at the

speech button on my machine, which I call **Swiftie**, and it speaks out loud, `'She thinks I'm idiotic.'`

Jack tells Miya how **Horrible Mrs Hare** spoke in that **loud**, slow voice this morning.

'You know the one people do when they think Ava can't understand them.'

Miya says, 'I knew it. Mrs Hare is actually horrible.'

Then the bell rings but Miya ignores it.

'Have you heard the **news**?'

Miya is speaking fast because break is over. 'It's **Sports Day** in four weeks.' Miya loves everything about sport. I'm not excited about Sports Day. Jack is not excited either.

Miya says, 'I could push you in a race, Ava?', and Jack says, 'Are you mad?'

Miya says, 'No,' and her face is all screwed up. It gets like this when she's cross. Jack says that Miya's not nearly sensible enough,

which makes Miya even more **cross**.

I know Jack wants to push me. Jack always pushes me. It's the job he's given himself. I'm waiting for what I know Miya is about to say to Jack.

'You're just not **fast** enough.'

'I will push her **safely**,' says Jack. He doesn't mind that he's not fast. Safety first, always.

Miya raises her eyebrows. 'But she wants to **WIN**. That's the whole point of a race!'

I look at Swiftie with my eyes. I select

each letter and then look at the speech button.

'Can I say something?' my trusty Swiftie speaks for me. Jack and Miya turn to me in **shock**.

I think they have actually **forgotten** I'm here.

Before I can say anything else, we have to get back to class.

TWINNING

Mrs Taylor (she's our deputy head) smiles at me as Jack wheels me past her. Jack doesn't stop. We might be late to class. Jack couldn't cope with being responsible for that.

Mrs Taylor calls back to us, 'Ava, can you stay in before lunch? I need to talk to you about something.'

I nod my head, which is my way of saying yes when everyone is in a hurry and it takes too long to use Swiftie.

Mrs Taylor and I have a **special** understanding. She has a brother with cerebral palsy. On my first day of school, Mrs Taylor came up to me and said, '**Hello Ava**.' She waited for me to say **'Hello'** back on Swiftie.

If she's walking past me, she always smiles, and if she thinks I'm looking gloomy, she says, '**Chin up, Ava.**'

I wonder what Mrs Taylor wants to talk to me about. I watch the clock all through class. It takes ages to get to lunch time. I can't **concentrate** because I keep thinking about what Mrs Taylor might say. Maybe she's having a baby. That would be **super** exciting.

I'm deep in thought when I see Martha

Brooks **whispering** something to her twin brother, Oliver. They sit in front of me and are always **planning** something. Once, Martha actually invited me over to her house. You would think we would have a lot to talk about, as we're both twins. But we don't. Maybe because I have an identical twin **sister** and she has a non-identical twin **brother**.

Just then, Mrs Taylor says she has some **big news**. Jack and Miya –

they sit next to me – look over and **raise** their eyebrows. This is what we have been waiting for.

Mrs Taylor tells us that we have a **new** girl joining us next week. She has moved to **London** all the way from **Australia**. This is a surprise. I don't know a single person from Australia. Mrs Taylor spins a **globe** – she points to England and then to Australia.

It's a long way away. Jack asks how long it takes to get there. Mrs Taylor says it takes 21 hours in a plane. **21 HOURS!** That's almost a **whole** day and a **whole** night.

Mrs Taylor says we must all help to look after her. She says it can be very **hard** starting a new school. Mrs Taylor looks around at all of us and then stares at Freddie. I hope Freddie is going to behave himself. The last new person we had in class ended up with a **frog** in his desk.

Freddie had found it in a pond and thought it was **HILARIOUS**. He was sent straight to Mrs Taylor's office. Mrs Taylor didn't laugh, and the new person never came back.

Freddie shrugs, and Mrs Taylor says, 'I'm **looking** at you, Freddie.' Just in case there was any doubt.

We all know it was really Albie. Freddie does exactly what Albie tells him to do. My mum would say they are as **thick as thieves**. They are always in **trouble** and always together.

The bell goes, and everyone races out to lunch, and Jack hovers next to me. Mrs Taylor tells him not to worry; she will wheel me down to lunch.

Mrs Taylor then tells me her unexpected news. It really is **BIG NEWS**. She says she wants me to look after the new girl. ME! To be honest, I'm so **surprised** by this. Even coming from Mrs Taylor. What if I scare the new girl with my wheelchair? I'm also secretly **delighted**. It's so cool to be asked to look after someone. Especially when

everyone is usually looking after me.

'Her name is Liv,' Mrs Taylor says. 'It's short for Olivia, but everyone calls her Liv.'

I have a **light bulb moment**. This is when you suddenly think of something really CLEVER. I tell Mrs Taylor that I can **change** my voice on Swiftie to have an **Australian** accent. I give her a demonstration, and Swiftie says, 'Good afternoon, Mrs Taylor,' in an Australian accent. Mrs Taylor

laughs a lot, and when she finally stops laughing, she says that if I want to change my voice, she thinks Liv will be delighted.

Mrs Taylor says Liv will start on **Tuesday**, which is tomorrow. It seems an odd time to start school. It's right in the middle of the term, and on a Tuesday. Why not on a Monday? Mr Dawson (he's our head teacher) is going to introduce Liv to the class first thing tomorrow morning.

Mr Dawson is the tallest man I have ever met. Everyone has to look up to Mr Dawson. I suppose this is a good thing when you are a head teacher. His hair sticks up, and he sometimes looks like he's just got out of bed. He says '**Exactly**' A LOT. The other day I said, `'Mr Dawson, I think koalas live in Australia,'` and he said, 'Exactly.' He makes you feel that you are right all the time. It's why we all like Mr Dawson.

Mrs Taylor says Liv is staying with her grandparents, who live in London.

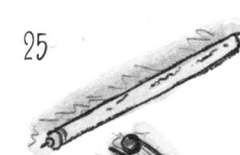

'Her parents will be here in four weeks, after Sports Day. She might be a little sad, missing her parents. I know you'll look after her, Ava.'

Mrs Taylor looks quite **serious**, which is not at all like Mrs Taylor. I nod my head to show I am taking my **huge** responsibilities seriously.

Mrs Taylor smiles, which is much more like Mrs Taylor. 'Good,' she says. 'Let's get you to lunch before there is nothing left to eat.'

TERRIFYING MUMMIES

After school, Flo, short for Florence, is gluing bits on her ancient Egypt project at the kitchen table. Flo is super **smart**, and she's my big sister. Flo is only older than me by a few minutes, but Mum always says Flo is the '**eldest**'. We are identical twins and are in the same year at school but in different classes.

Last weekend, Mum took us to the Tutankhamun exhibition at the British Museum. It's to do with **ancient Egypt**. Flo likes to have extra information for her school projects.

It was a **big** event, as we had to go by tube. Mum is always good at working out which tube stops we can go to with my wheelchair. We have to use '**accessible**' stations. On the tube map, they usually have a wheelchair sign next to accessible stations. Mum always has to call the station on the day we travel just in case the lift in the accessible station is broken. This did happen once, and Mum was **FURIOUS**.

When we're on the tube, Flo sometimes gets upset that people stare at me, but I've got used to it. Mostly everyone is always super **helpful**.

The trip on the tube was the most exciting part of the day. It's always an adventure. Someone got on the tube at Green Park and started playing the saxophone,

and everyone just kept looking down at their phones. He was only on the tube for two stops and then got off at Leicester Square. Then it was only one more stop to Covent Garden, which has a lift because, to get out of the station, there is a **spiral** staircase with 193 steps. Mum says that even people who are not in wheelchairs find them impossible to climb.

At the exhibition, Flo spent ages looking at old stone statues, and I just wanted to get back on the tube.

Ancient Egypt gives me the creeps. We saw lots of mummies, but they're not what you think. These mummies look like ghosts wrapped in white bandages. They are not at all like our mummy. Thank goodness. We would be **scared** out of our wits.

Flo looks up from her project but says nothing. She's busy making everything perfect. I look at Swiftie. **'Mrs Hare was horrible today.'**

Flo shrugs. I know what she's thinking, but she says it out loud anyway. 'Sometimes people are horrible, Ava, and sometimes it's not just because you're in a wheelchair. Mrs Hare is **horrible** to everyone.'

This simply cannot be true. Mrs Hare would not be horrible to Flo. Teachers love Flo, and she's never ever in **trouble**. She's always so good. Not like Freddie and Albie.

Flo is listening to music. It's a girl band I haven't heard before.

She listens to music a lot, mostly in her room. 'It's because she's older than you,' Mum says, walking into the kitchen.

'By four minutes!' I say, looking at a button on Swiftie and turning up the volume so she shouts my words.

Sometimes Flo's music is so loud I can't hear myself think. I once heard Mrs Taylor say that when Freddie and Albie were **making a racket**.

Flo pays absolutely no attention to my loud words – she's looking at two sheets of gold paper with her

concentration face on. Holding the paper up, she asks, 'Which one?' They both look exactly the same, but I don't say this. I don't want to be 'idiotic', like Mrs Hare thinks I am.

'The right one,' I say.

Flo puts the left sheet down on the table and starts cutting out cats. She's using the sheet of paper I chose. I must

have made a good choice as Flo doesn't always agree with me.

I don't know why she's making cats from gold paper. Maybe Egyptians love gold cats?

Mum starts putting the shopping away in the cupboards.

'I passed Jack and Miya's mums running today. It must be **exhausting** – all that running.'

Flo looks at me and we smile at the same time. Mum can never see the point in all that 'running'. She's constantly saying things like 'They'll wear out their knees'. I think this means they won't have any knees left? I don't think Mum is right. Jack and Miya's mums look like they can run forever.

Mum sits between us at the kitchen table. 'It looks **amazing**, Flo.'

We all stare at the very gold and **glittery** project. The kitchen table is covered in glitter, and when Mum drinks her tea, the bottom of her mug has glitter all over it.

I start laughing.

'What?' she says.

'You have glitter on your face.' Flo points to Mum's face.

'Nothing like a bit of **sparkle** at this time of the afternoon,' Mum says, smiling. She puts her hand in the glitter and then smears it on my face. We are all **laughing** so hard we don't **hear** the doorbell.

THE SCHOOL GOSSIP

Jack is at the front door holding a furry toy **koala**.

'I found this in the cupboard at home. It's for Liv,' Jack says **proudly**, walking into the kitchen.

'Who's Liv?' Mum asks. Flo doesn't have to ask. She already knows.

Everyone at school knows. It's the school **GOSSIP**.

I gaze at Swiftie. Some days I just need her to go faster. I'm so excited to tell Mum my BIG NEWS.

`'She's a new girl–'`

Before I can finish, Jack **blurts** it out. 'Ava's been put in charge of her.'

'Really?' Flo looks surprised. This is news to Flo. It makes me feel **IMPORTANT**.

Flo is always the one with the big news, but today, it's my turn.

'Yes, REALLY. What's so surprising about that?'

I wish Swiftie had a cross voice. In this moment, she sounds rather too friendly. It sort of **DEFLATES** my crossness. Swiftie sounds like the voice on Mum's phone that gives her directions in the car. There is no cross voice, no sad voice and no happy voice. It's just all so the **SAME**.

Thankfully, Flo does get the point, even without the cross voice.

She says there is no need to get **ANGSTY**.

And then Mum says she wants to know all about it. Jack opens his mouth to say something and then looks at me. He can see I'm trying to say something, so he closes his mouth again.

Swiftie speaks for me. **'She's from Australia.'**

Flo looks at the koala. She arches an eyebrow. I wish Flo hadn't given Jack the **LOOK**.

'I know, I know.' Jack is all in a **fluster**, trying to hide the koala under the table.

It's obvious we're way too old to

play with a toy koala, but I hadn't said anything to Jack because he has **FEELINGS**. I know this because we are **BEST FRIENDS**.

I glare at Swiftie and write the words as fast as I can. `'I think it will make Liv feel at home.'`

I give Flo an **angry** stare and hope she gets the message. I think she does because she leaves, and I hear her going up the stairs. She's **stamping** her feet hard. It's not as if I can go up the stairs after her.

My bedroom is wheelchair-friendly. That's what everyone says. It's downstairs because I can't walk upstairs. I think my room is really supposed to be a study.

Mum **sighs** and cuts a slice of **cake** for each of us. Mum always says a slice of cake and a cup of tea make everyone **feel better**. She's right too. Once, we had cake when Flo broke her arm.

She fell off a slide in the park and had to go to hospital and get a plaster on her arm. Not a little plaster, like when you graze yourself. A **ginormous** plaster that is all up your arm. It was covered in drawings her friends had done to **cheer** her up.

Jack sits at the kitchen table eating his cake. I can see he's feeling better already. The koala is forgotten. I can't stop thinking about Liv. I need to come up with something **FUN**. Jack says he thinks we should have all our 'Liv'

YUMMY

meetings at my house, which I know is because of the cake.

I **gaze** at Swiftie. `'We need to think of something special to do with Liv.'`

Flo appears again. She must have been sitting on the top step, listening. She does this sometimes. I don't smile at her. I want her to know I'm still **cross** with her.

'Why don't you do something on **Sports Day**?'

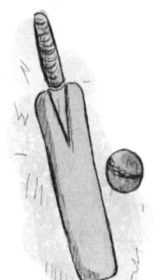  

Flo says we could have two teams – **England** and **Australia**. Like in the cricket. Liv could captain Team Australia. Each team could wear the country's colours.

Flo always comes up with the best plan. It's maddening, especially when I'm still **CROSS** with her.

Jack is bursting with excitement. He says we can use the koala as the mascot for the Australian team. I'm not sure about this but he says we can dress it up in **green** and **gold**. The colours of

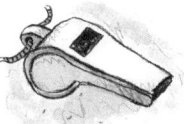  

Australia. A yellow T-shirt and green scarf.

Jack is a **genius**. I'm impressed he knows the Australian colours. He knows lots of things you wouldn't think are important. But actually, they are **super** important. He always says these important things right at the **perfect** moment.

The toy koala was not such a bad idea after all.

I'm still thinking about the green and gold. Where will we get green and gold clothes small enough for the koala?

Flo says we might find something in the charity shop. She says charity shops always have loads of baby clothes. Sometimes I think Flo can **read my mind**. I didn't even ask the question out loud.

'Just one thing,' Flo says. 'You will need to tell Mrs Taylor your **plans**. She's the Sports Day organiser.'

'**Okay,**' I say, pleased to have a mission.

We already have a plan, and Liv hasn't even arrived yet. I hope she **likes** me.

THE NEW GIRL

On Tuesday morning, Jack is wheeling me around the corner, but in his **excitement**, we practically run over Mrs Hare.

'You again,' she says. 'Do you mind?' She **spits** out her words when she's talking. 'Look where you are going.'

Jack looks at the floor.
'Sorry, Mrs Hare.'

'I should think so,' she says back.

Miya is behind Mrs Hare, pretending she's spitting when talking. I'm trying really hard not to **laugh**. But it doesn't work. As soon as Mrs Hare disappears around the corner, I'm in fits of **giggles**.

There is something different about Mrs Hare today, and I'm trying to work out what it is. Then, I know ...

She's not wearing her Velcro shoes. Today, she has bright red tights and shiny, black lace-up shoes. It must be

a **special** occasion. I wonder what the occasion is?

Jack quickly wheels me into the classroom, followed by Miya, who is still pretending to spit like Mrs Hare.

'Time for class,' Miya whispers, as she showers us with spit, causing me to get the giggles again.

Just as we are about to start class, Mrs Taylor walks in, and Mrs Hare looks **cross** at the interruption.

She sighs and puts her pen down on the desk.

'Good morning, class,' Mrs Taylor says, smiling at us.

'Morning,' we respond. I don't because it would take too long and Mrs Taylor knows I'm saying 'Morning' anyway.

This is the moment Mrs Taylor told me about. She tells the class that we have to be on our **best** behaviour this morning. Mr Dawson will be introducing us to Liv, the new girl.

I can't believe I'm really about to

meet Liv for the first time. I think she probably has **blonde** hair from all the sun in Australia. And probably **freckles** – from all the **sun**, obviously.

I asked Mum to help me put on my **favourite** black-and-pink hair clips for the special occasion.
I hope Liv likes
my hair clips. Mrs Taylor
said we're going to be **buddies** and I'm responsible for taking Liv to break, lunch and class.

Then Mrs Taylor gives us a **warning**

look just before Mr Dawson walks in with Liv. Everyone in the class goes **quiet**, even Freddie and Albie. Mr Dawson is wearing a **tie**, which he never does, and Liv is standing next to him.

Liv has **blonde** hair – I was right. She's so tall my neck hurts when I look up at her. She has **enormous dangly earrings** in her ears. These are definitely **NOT** allowed. They must have **different** school rules in Australia.

'Let's give Liv a **warm** welcome, shall we?'

This is what Mr Dawson always says every time someone new comes to visit the school.

We all say together, 'Welcome,' and Liv looks rather **startled**.

Mrs Taylor asks me to come to the front and introduce myself. Jack wheels me over to the front of the class where Liv is standing.

I look at Swiftie, and she says the message I had already saved. **'Hello, I'm Ava. Welcome to our class.'**

'Hello,' Liv says quietly.

'You're sitting at the desk next to Ava,' Mrs Taylor explains. 'You can follow her now.'

Liv follows Jack and me back to my desk. I smile towards the empty desk next to me, and Liv sits down. Miya gives me a **thumbs up**.

When Mr Dawson and Mrs Taylor leave the room, Mrs Hare starts teaching us the most **boring** lesson ever. It's a **science** lesson. She keeps talking about seeds

and germination or maybe it's Germany. I can't work it out. Liv looks worried and I don't blame her. She probably has her lessons on the beach every day.

The radiators are on full blast today even though it's the middle of summer. The classroom is so **stuffy**. Mum says we're having a cold spell. Liv must think she's in a **SAUNA**. I know all about saunas because

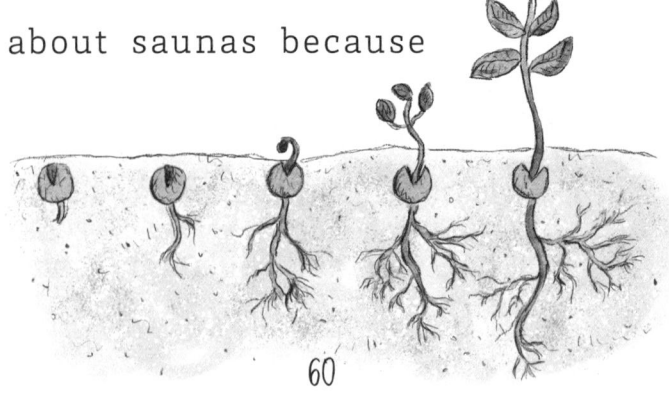

Mum sometimes goes on wellness breaks. She says they give her extra **energy** to keep going. In Mum's photos, they always have a swimming pool and a sauna. Mum never really seems to have more energy after her break. She always has to keep going back.

I don't hear anything Mrs Hare says about seeds. I'm watching Liv look miserable and I'm so worried my head starts to hurt. What am I going to do?

THE SO-COOL DANGLY EARRINGS

The bell goes for break time, and Jack and Miya come to my desk. They **bump** into everyone trying to get out of the classroom. Liv looks like she might burst into **tears**. I definitely can't mention the dangly earrings.

Miya whispers in my ear, 'She's so cool.' Miya is

looking at the rule-breaking earrings. Liv is still sitting, her **earrings** dangling from her ears. Everyone else has left the classroom for break time. I'm not sure what to do . . .

Freddie turns around at the classroom door. 'Coming?' He **smirks**.

As if Liv even knows where to go. Freddie doesn't wait as he runs out after Albie.

'It's break time, Liv. Do you want to come outside with us?'

When I look at the speech button and Swiftie speaks, Liv **jumps** like she has had a shock.

Miya takes her **OPPORTUNITY**. She leads Liv behind me so she can see my machine. 'Ava talks using her machine – Swiftie is like a computer but better. Ava looks at the alphabet with her eyes, and Swiftie then writes the words,' Miya says **IMPORTANTLY**.

It's an odd thing, being talked about when you are actually there. Miya knows I hate it. But how else do you explain Swiftie? Liv nods her head but doesn't speak.

Jack gets up and **leads** the way. 'Let's go to the **den**,' he says confidently.

Maybe Liv will speak in the den. I'm starting to think she might **HATE** us.

'The den is our place,' Miya excitedly explains to a silent Liv.

Actually, it's just the place where we sit under a shady tree at break time. Miya is trying to make it into a **BIG DEAL**.

When we get to the DEN, we sit in a little circle and nobody speaks. Mrs

Taylor should never have put me in charge. It's all going horribly wrong.

'There you are,' Mrs Taylor says, suddenly appearing from nowhere. I have never been so **happy** to see a teacher.

She asks Liv how she is getting along, and then Liv says, 'Well, thank you.' And then we are all shocked. Liv sounds **different**. It's the first time we have heard her speak more than one word. She sounds **funny**. Her voice goes up at the end of each word.

Miya looks at me as if to say, she sounds different. And I nod to say, I know.

Jack can't help himself. 'Why do you sound like that?' he asks Liv.

I **roll** my eyes at Miya. It's **so** Jack.

Mrs Taylor says Liv has an Australian accent. It sounds slightly different from the way we speak. It's like Americans have an American accent in films. It's the same thing in Australia.

`'Like this.'` I look at Swiftie, who speaks, `'Like this,'` in an Australian accent. Everybody laughs because I sound so funny. Even Liv laughs a little bit.

'That's right,' Mrs Taylor says, and then she starts telling off Freddie, who has just thrown a ball at someone's head. Mrs Taylor walks off to sort it all out.

The break bell goes and our time in the **DEN** is over. It's such hard work being a **buddy**. I'm not sure I'm very good at it at all.

Oliver and Martha Brooks are **whispering** as they walk past us. They look at Liv like she's from another planet and giggle. Liv looks like she might cry.

Last year, they invited me to their **party**. Martha let me go into her bedroom – her bedroom is downstairs, which is why I was able to go in it. She has the **biggest** bed I have ever seen. Not even my mum has a bed as big as Martha's. She has curtains around her bed that you can see through and **fairy lights** above the bed. It looks like a princess bed. I would **LOVE** Martha's bed. Just when I was thinking that if I had a bed that size, Miya could sleep in my bed when she has **sleepovers**, Martha did something I simply couldn't believe. She pressed a button, and at the end of her bed, a **TV** appeared. A real TV! Her bedroom is **HEAVEN**.

Martha's mum works in TV, which is why I think they have so many TVs, practically one in every room in their house, and I didn't even go upstairs. At the party, Martha's mum organised a dance-off. She put really loud music on, and there was a **disco ball** with coloured lights hanging from the ceiling. Then Martha's fabulous mum started dancing with everyone. She really is the **coolest**.

We walk back to the classroom, ignoring Oliver and Martha Brooks because of their **RUDENESS**.

Jack pushes me in my wheelchair. I think we really need to try and cheer Liv up.

Miya and I look at each other, and then Miya says, 'We're going back to Ava's house after school. Do you want to come over?'

I am slightly in a **panic** about this because I haven't asked Mum. There is so much to think about when you're a **BUDDY**. My head is permanently full of stuff I need to do.

Liv looks rather worried about coming over, but she says, 'I'll ask my granny,' in her **funny** voice.

I still haven't mentioned the dangly earrings. That will have to wait. As Mum would say, I need to find the **right** moment.

TEAM AUSTRALIA

When I get home, I tell Mum everything and she starts to get **BUSY** in the kitchen. She says she's preparing tea for everyone.

I'm not sure if Liv is coming. I hope Mum won't be upset if she doesn't come.

'She'll be here,' Flo says. Yet again Flo knows exactly what I'm thinking.

It's like she's **TELEPATHIC**. I don't even need to speak. She knows my thoughts. Sort of like **magic**. Sometimes, this is a good thing. Sometimes, it's a bad thing.

Jack's koala is sitting on the kitchen table and Miya is busy writing notes. She has yellow sticky notes all over the table. She is planning Sports Day. Miya says this is exactly what Liv needs – all Australians like to be **outside**. She knows this because her dad has a sister who lives in Sydney.

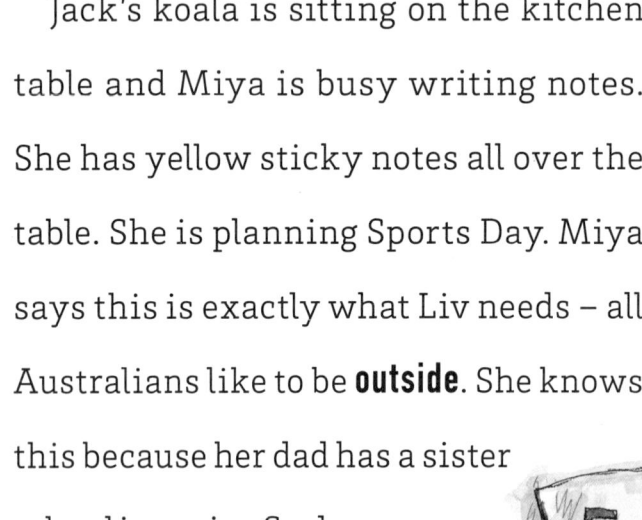

Her cousins are always swimming in the pool or at the beach. The swimming pool is in the garden of her cousins' actual house.

I hope Miya is right about this.

The doorbell rings, and Miya races to the front door, followed by Mum.

I hear Mum say, 'Hello,' and ask, 'Would you like to come inside?' Mum has her most **polite** voice on. It's the voice she uses when she comes to parent meetings at the school.

'No, I must be off.' That must be Liv's granny. 'I'll be back in an hour.' She doesn't sound very Australian.

'Perfect. I'm Sarah,' Mum says. 'We'll take good care of Liv, I promise.'

Miya is so **excited** that Liv has actually come. She walks into the kitchen with Liv and looks so pleased with herself. Like she's won a prize.

Liv stares at the table. Mum has taken away all the yellow sticky notes, and there is **ABSOLUTELY** no fruit to be seen. Instead, there are biscuits and cakes and juice on the table. We are never usually allowed **TREATS**, but it's the second time this week.

I must remember to thank Mum. It's such an effort. I hope Liv likes it.

'Come and sit down, Liv.' Mum fusses. 'It must be very hard not having your parents here.'

Liv nods and says nothing. She looks so sad – I think she must be homesick. I don't know what I would do without my mum.

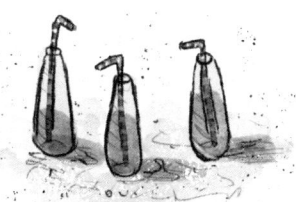

Mum gives everyone a little paper plate. It's like we are having a proper party. I'm so nervous I can't eat anything, but Jack takes a **cupcake** straight away and offers Liv one too. Miya is far too busy preparing her notes to eat anything.

Then Miya announces, rather too loudly, 'This is our Sports Day planning party.'

She seems to be **IN CHARGE** now and I don't mind at all. It is sometimes quite tiring being in charge of someone.

'Sports Day?' Liv says, and we are

SPORTS DAY!

all so shocked she has spoken. She has actually **SPOKEN**. **WORDS**. And no one even asked her a question. Even Jack stops eating his cupcake.

'It's in four weeks,' Miya says.

We are all looking at each other. Me, Miya and Jack. This is what Mrs Taylor would call **PROGRESS**.

Flo walks in and grabs a biscuit.

'Oh, hi Liv,' she says as if they are best friends.

'Hi,' Liv speaks again. I just don't know how Flo does it. Everyone **KNOWS** her. Everyone **LOVES** her.

'How's the Sports Day plan going?' Flo says to all of us.

Liv answers, 'We have Sports Day in Australia. It's fun.' We can't believe we are hearing this. It's like a **MIRACLE**. Liv talking and in proper sentences.

Miya keeps going. She doesn't want Liv to stop with the **COMMUNICATION**. That's a word I hear a lot. My speech pathologist says it all the time.

'Ava, you have to **communicate**.

Ava, use your words', she is always saying.

Sometimes you just don't want to communicate. Liv would be on my side. I think my speech pathologist might find Liv a **CHALLENGE**. She would have a thing or two to say to Liv.

'What do you do on your Sports Day?' Miya asks.

Liv then says something that makes us all quite worried. At least Jack and I are worried when Liv says, 'I like **running**.'

This could be very **BAD** news indeed. Liv could be **COMPETITION** and Miya is SO competitive. She always has to come **first**. In my bedroom, I have books. In Miya's bedroom, she has **medals**. She likes the gold ones the best.

'I hate running,' Jack says.

'We know,' Miya and I both say together.

I'm not at all sure about **SPORTS DAY** now.

It might be just about the **WORST** plan ever.

Miya has all her sticky notes in her hands. There are hundreds of them. Some of them only have one word on them. One says '**FAST**'; another one says '**COLOURS**'.

Miya explains her idea to Liv. Really, it was Flo's idea, but I say nothing. Miya says we are thinking of naming our teams after **countries**. And that Liv would be in the Australian team. Jack looks at me, and I know we are thinking the same thing.

Liv and Miya will be running against each other. This is **VERY BAD** news indeed.

DETENTION

It's the start of a new week and we have lots to do.

'MIYA MURANO,' Mrs Hare shouts, and I **jump** in my wheelchair. Her voice is so loud. 'Will you pay attention?'

Miya has the best name ever.

It sounds like the name of a movie star. Her dad is Japanese, and he is ultra-polite. I have only ever seen him wearing a suit and tie. Jack and I have to call him Mr Murano. I have no idea what his first name is.

My name, Ava Spark, is utterly terrible. Mrs Taylor doesn't agree. She says it's a **brilliant** name.

'You are a **bright spark**,' she said to me once. 'Full of **energy** and **enthusiasm**, so it's the perfect name for you.'

I'm not so sure.

I would much rather have a name that sounds like a movie star.

I can see Miya is writing notes – AGAIN.

Mrs Hare comes right up close to Miya to look at what she is doing. She **squeaks** in her shoes from the front of the classroom to Miya's desk.

Miya puts a piece of paper over her notes so Mrs Hare can't see.

Mrs Hare says, 'Miya,' and a little bit of spit comes out of her mouth. It falls on Jack's arm and he wipes it off with a

tissue. 'You will be staying in at break time.'

Today Mrs Hare looks even crosser than normal. Miya **rolls** her eyes and Mrs Hare **ignores** her.

Luckily, we make it through to break time without any further **INCIDENT**.

At break, we decide to stay in the classroom with Miya to keep her company. Mrs Hare lets us, which is a surprise. She even looks over Miya's shoulder and says, 'Good idea. You should tell Mrs Taylor about your plan.'

Then she sits back down and starts reading a book. So, Miya writes a list for me:

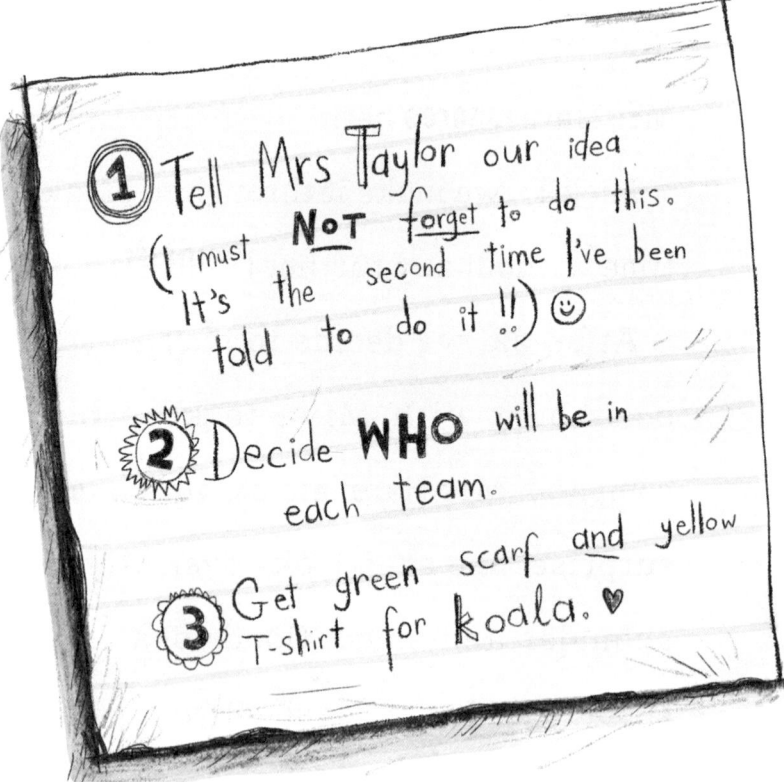

1. Tell Mrs Taylor our idea (I must **NOT** forget to do this. It's the second time I've been told to do it !!) ☺

2. Decide **WHO** will be in each team.

3. Get green scarf and yellow T-shirt for koala. ♥

There is quite a lot to do but I don't say I can't do it. Mum is always saying 'You have to rise to the **challenge**'.

She says this when there is something difficult Flo or I have to do. And when we don't want to do it. She says this quite a lot in the mornings. At 7.30am, when we are not ready to leave, she sighs and says, 'Let's rise to the challenge this morning, girls, and try and be on time.'

Miya says she will be **responsible** for getting printable race bibs. She says everyone has to have a number on their

T-shirt like in proper races. I think she must have got this information from her mum. It must be something her mum knows about from running in the London Marathon.

Jack also has responsibilities. Miya has given them to him. He will now be pushing me in my wheelchair. Miya says she can't do it as she needs to **CONSERVE** her energy for the **BIG RACE** and she can't run twice.

It's a **huge** job, organising an event.

Miya is in the middle of telling us

what to do. Then a miracle happens. Liv is actually **smiling**.

Mrs Taylor appears. She has a habit of appearing out of nowhere, and says she has heard about our idea. She thinks our Sports Day plan is simply **brilliant**. And Mrs Taylor is almost always right.

I think Mrs Hare told Mrs Taylor about our idea. I can now tick it off my to-do list.

Mrs Taylor looks at our plan properly and says, 'What a brilliant idea.'

Then Freddie and Albie come running

into class.

We all stare at them like they are aliens.

Albie says to me, 'We just want to make sure we are in **TEAM ENGLAND**.'

And then Freddie says, 'NOT **Team Australia**. Just to be **clear**.'

And I say, **'OKAY,'** because this might just be the perfect plan.

After Freddie and Albie have run off, Miya whispers, 'They are terrible runners.'

And I say, **'I know.'**

Now there are four runners in each team. The rest of the class will be our cheer squad.

I've sorted out the teams so that Liv and Miya are in the same team. Thank goodness. I write the teams down on Swiftie and press save. I'll tell Miya at our next meeting.

We organise another meeting for Friday after school. I still have one more thing on my list to do. I need to find a yellow T-shirt and green scarf for our koala mascot.

THE HOUSE IS UNDER WATER

After school on Friday, I arrive home with Jack, and Mum is running around the house, **shouting**, 'How many times have I told you?!' Flo's face is all puffy like she's been crying.

Our sitting room looks like it's an actual river. There is **water** everywhere. Mum and Flo are putting towels down all over the floor. Suddenly, drops of water land on my head. It's raining inside our house. There is water **dripping** through our ceiling onto the floor.

'Into the kitchen and out of the way,' Mum shouts at me.

She's waving her hands like she's **shooing** a fly away. It's hard for me to get out of the way because I'm in my wheelchair. I decide this is not a good time to point this out to Mum.

This is a **DISASTER**. The wet carpet is really smelly. There are no treats today.

Just Mum saying words she really shouldn't be saying. If Liv's granny hears Mum's words, Liv will be banned from my house **FOREVER**.

The doorbell rings and Miya is standing at the door.

'Something **smells** really **bad**.' Miya is sniffing the air as she walks into the house.

'It's a flood,' Jack says.

'A what?' Miya says.

'**A FLOOD.**' I put Swiftie on **full** volume.

'Oh,' Miya says, looking confused.

Flo walks into the kitchen, rubbing her eyes.

'What happened?' I ask.

Flo says in a **squeaky** voice, 'I left the bath water running and it overflowed.'

Miya nods. 'My mum did that once. All the water poured out of the bath onto the floor and through the ceiling. There was a big **wet** patch for ages on the ceiling. We had to have the decorators in.'

None of this sounds good. Mum is

always saying she's stretched to the limit. She will not be able to afford decorators.

Flo starts crying again.

Mum shouts, 'Flo, where are you?' and Flo runs back to the sitting room. I hear Mum say one of the **bad** words again and then the doorbell goes.

'Don't worry,' Miya says as she races out to get the door.

Miya brings Liv into the kitchen. 'Liv's granny dropped her off and waved from the car.'

I know why she's telling me this and I feel better. It means that Liv's granny would not have heard Mum's shouting from the car.

Liv doesn't say hello, but she's holding a packet of **biscuits**. As we have no food in the house at all, I'm quite pleased to see the biscuits. Jack shuts the kitchen door so we can't hear all the shouting. Liv is looking around with a **worried** look on her face.

Thankfully, all is **calm** in the kitchen. It also smells better with the door closed.

Miya says we need to get on with things. We only have **TWO WEEKS** to go before Sports Day. She opens her bag and gets out lots of pieces of paper with numbers on them and holds them up for us to admire. 'Every person in the team needs one of these,' she says.

Jack asks, 'How are they going to stick on our T-shirts?'

Miya frowns and then Liv says, 'We can use safety pins.

We can punch holes in the paper at both ends for the safety pins.'

Miya says that this is a **fantastic** idea. Liv smiles shyly and Jack then says that his mum always writes her name under her number so that the crowd cheering her on shout out her name.

We agree that we should definitely do this. We are making real **PROGRESS**.

In our relay race, each member of the team has to run once. Miya says we have to think about the order of the race. Who will run first and who will run last. I show her my list, which I have already done in order and saved on Swiftie.

Team Australia	Team England
Miya	Albie
Jack, me	Oliver
Flo	Martha
Liv	Freddie

Miya looks at the list and **smiles**. I'm pleased she thinks it's okay.

Mum walks into the kitchen and she seems to have calmed down. Although she's probably just on her **best** behaviour because of Liv being a guest in the house.

She makes herself a cup of
tea, which she says is to
CALM HER NERVES. I think it's
working. Flo's face is less puffy
now and she comes to sit with us.

Flo looks at the list we have made for our relay team. 'I like it,' she says. It's great to have approval from my **BIG SISTER**. 'Liv, you're going to have to run fast,' Flo says, and I can see Liv feels the **PRESSURE**.

'I will,' Liv says. 'I'll make sure I bring my **esky** with drinks for after the race.

Mum always does that in Australia.'

And we all look at her with a frown because we don't know what an **esky** is.

Flo speaks for all of us, 'What's an **esky**?'

'It's to keep drinks cool,' Liv says with a shrug.

Flo is still confused. She types into her phone: `What's an esky?` Flo was allowed a phone this year – it's Mum's old phone.

'Esky,' Flo says, sounding important, 'is from the word "Eskimo", a person who lives in the Arctic, where it's cold. It's a "cooler bag".'

It might not be hot like it is in Australia in the summer. Mostly it rains on Sports Day, but I don't say this to Liv. She seems **excited** about her cooler bag.

DISASTER STRIKES

One week later, everyone is racing out for break time, and I see something sticking out from Martha's desk. It's a mini Union Jack **flag**. I should have thought of this already.

I don't know where I'm going to get Australian flags from in London. In the **DEN**, I tell Jack, Miya and Liv about the

flag problem.

Liv says, 'No worries,' which is something Australians say a lot. She says she has some mini flags she can bring from her granny's house. I'm so relieved because we need flags being waved for Team Australia.

I pull out Miya's list and take a look:

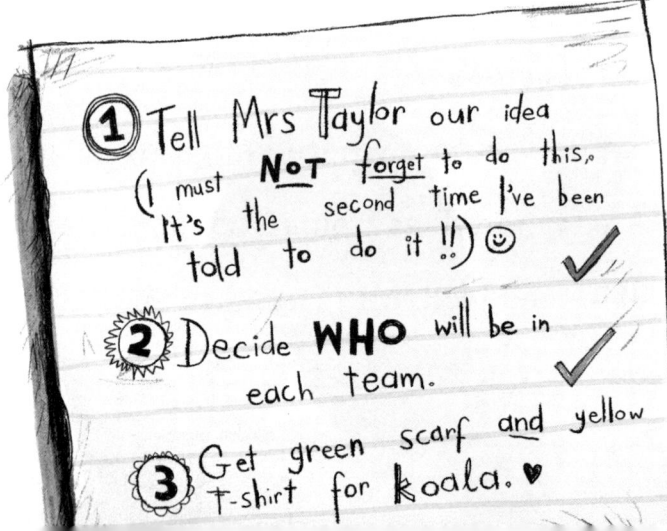

① Tell Mrs Taylor our idea (I must **NOT** forget to do this. It's the second time I've been told to do it !!) ☺ ✓

② Decide **WHO** will be in each team. ✓

③ Get green scarf and yellow t-shirt for koala. ♥

Flo meets Jack and me by the school gate at the end of the day. We are on a mission to find a **green** scarf and **yellow** T-shirt for our koala mascot. It's the **final** thing to do on the list.

Jack wheels me, and Flo walks alongside.

'Mrs Murano said she will be volunteering in the charity shop today and she will help us find what we need,' Jack says. Mrs Murano is much **louder** than Mr Murano. Everyone knows her because she is always running, training for a marathon. She says we must call her Annie. 'None of this silly Mrs Murano business.'

'Hello!' Annie waves at us as we come down the street.

'Hello Annie,' Jack and Flo say at the same time.

Annie looks down at the three steps to get into the charity shop. 'Oh dear,' she says.

'Don't worry,' I say. **'I can wait outside.'** I'm trying to make Annie feel better because she looks really upset.

'You will do no such thing,' Annie says with a frown on her face. Then she gets **busy**.

'Jack, you stay with Ava. Flo, you come with me.' Flo follows Annie, and Jack waits with me.

Before we know it, Annie and Flo appear at the door with two **long** planks of wood.

'We found these out by the rubbish at the back of the shop,' Flo says excitedly.

Jack helps Annie and Flo put the

wooden planks down from the top of the steps to the pavement.

'We have to make sure they are the right distance apart,' says Annie, 'so that we can keep the wheels on the two planks.'

Jack takes a look. 'I think it's right.'

'It's a bit steep,' Annie says. 'Jack, why don't you and I **push** Ava up the planks. Flo, you stay at the top and make sure the planks stay **stable**.'

Everyone gets in position.

'Are we ready?' asks Annie.

'**Ready!**' say Jack and Flo. Then I feel myself being **pushed** up a hill by Annie and Jack, who is panting slightly. When I arrive at the top of the steps into the shop, Flo quickly moves away so I don't run over her.

'Well, there we are,' says Annie. 'You made it!' She puts her hands on her hips and looks at the ramp we have made. 'I must talk to our manager about getting a ramp. It's no good at all that you can't get into the shop.'

I have never been into the shop before.

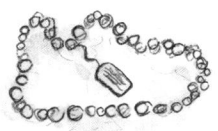

There are so many things to see – clothes, jewellery, bags, hats, even umbrellas. It's like a **treasure** trove of unexpected things.

'Now tell me exactly what it is you need?' Annie says, looking at me. Flo and Jack wait for me to answer.

`'We need a small yellow T-shirt for our koala mascot.'`

Jack pulls the koala out of the bag.

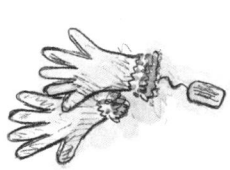

'And a green scarf.'

'Oh yes, Miya told me about Sports Day. It sounds like fun.'

Just then Miya arrives all out of breath. 'I'm sorry I'm late. Mrs Hare made me stay in.'

I'm worried Miya is about to be told off, but instead, Annie says, 'You missed all the **drama**.'

Miya looks at the wooden planks at the door. 'I can see,' she says.

'Right, I think I've found just what you're looking for.' Annie appears with a

tiny yellow T-shirt and a very long scarf that would go around the koala about five times.

Annie sees my worried face. 'Don't worry, Ava, we can cut the scarf so it's just the right size.' She then uses a pair of **scissors**, and it is perfect. Our Aussie koala is ready to go.

'**Brilliant**, Mum – thank you.' Miya gives her mum a hug.

'Are you coming to Sports Day?' I ask Annie.

'I wouldn't miss it,' she says.

'We better get going,' Flo says.

'Alright, you lot, time to go then. Flo and Jack, why don't you push Ava down the wooden planks, and Miya and I will stand on the pavement at the bottom of the planks, just to make sure the wheelchair doesn't start going at speed down the road.'

Annie and Miya stand with their

hands out, ready to catch me. I feel a **rush** of wind against my face as my wheelchair goes down the planks at **speed** and into Annie and Miya's arms.

'We've got you,' they say, and my wheelchair comes to a stop.

'I'm definitely going to have a talk with my manager about this,' Annie says again.

'Thank you,' I say to Annie. We head back home, the four of us with our koala mascot.

THE BIG RACE

It's the morning of the **big** race and I have **butterflies** in my tummy. I was awake at 5.30am this morning, which never happens. Mum is so surprised when Flo and I are in the kitchen in our yellow T-shirts and ready to leave at 7.30am. She says it's a 'first'.

'Have you even had breakfast, girls?' she asks. 'You can't run on an empty stomach.'

'Already done, Mum,' Flo says. We had our breakfast at 6am! 'We need to go,' Flo adds.

'Well, then, let's get you to school.'

Mum is wearing the **strangest** hat I have ever seen. She says it's called a **cork hat**. It has corks hanging off it. When her head moves, the corks swing. She says this stops insects going into her mouth.

Apparently, this is something that happens in Australia because of all the flies in the **hot** weather.

When we arrive at school, everyone else is already there. Jack, Miya and Liv are wearing their yellow T-shirts for Team Australia. We all have our bibs on with our numbers and our names underneath. Liv has even taken out her dangly earrings. I'm relieved as Mrs Taylor would say they are a **HAZARD**, and I don't want Liv getting into trouble.

The entire school is **watching** our relay.

Half are in yellow for **Team Australia**, and half in red for **Team England**. I can see Mum at the front with a group of parents. She is waving one of the mini flags Liv gave us. She catches my eye and waves at me.

Mr Dawson is standing at the starting line. He is wearing a black tracksuit. He says he has gone casual on account of Sports Day.

'Are we ready?' Mr Dawson shouts.

We all nod. We are too **nervous** to answer with words.

Then Mrs Taylor says over the loudspeaker, 'Everyone take their places for the Team Australia and Team England relay.'

My hands are sweaty, and my heart is **pounding**.

We all take our places and then Mr Dawson says, 'Ready ... Set ... **Go!**'

Miya is off running, and everyone is shouting like mad. Miya is in the lead.

Albie is close behind her. She is running towards us, and Jack has to tap her hand before we can go. I can hear everyone **cheering** and **yelling** my name. Then I see Mrs Hare waving an Australian flag. She's in a yellow T-shirt and is smiling. I can hear Jack panting and Oliver runs past us. Flo is waiting at the end. Jack taps her hand and she starts running. Martha passes her and Team

England is in the lead when Flo taps Liv. There is so much noise; all I can hear are Liv and Freddie's names being chanted. Liv and Freddie are running next to each other, then Liv suddenly goes **faster**, and she's in the lead and the noise of the crowd cheering is so **loud** and Liv just makes it ... **winning** the relay.

Liv is panting so hard from all the running. Freddie goes up to her and shakes her hand and **congratulates** her even though he looks a bit sad. Jack wheels me over to Liv and we all crowd around her, giving her three cheers for running so fast.

Jack hands Liv the koala and Mum gives an **enormous** Australian flag to Liv, who wraps it around herself. Liv runs around the track, and everyone is cheering and waving flags as she waves back at them.

Mr Dawson makes an announcement over the loudspeaker.

'**Team Australia** is the winner. Congratulations to both teams. Please can Team Australia and Team England make their way to the podium.'

There is a ramp set up, which Jack uses to wheel me onto the podium.

'Quiet please for the **medal** ceremony,' Mr Dawson says, and everyone stops cheering. Mr Dawson puts a medal around each one of us and shakes our hands. He then says, 'Please congratulate the teams.'

As I look at the crowd, I see that Mrs Hare is standing next to Mrs Taylor and they are both cheering. Annie is next to Mum. I think maybe Annie found the cork hat for Mum in the charity shop.

We shake hands with Team England, and even though Martha, Oliver, Albie and Freddie didn't win, they don't seem to mind. It's been what Mum would call a 'bonding exercise'. We are all friends again.

Liv says it's one of the **best** days of her life and flings her arms around me in a

bear hug. We all then **huddle** together and pat each other on the back. We decide to meet up tomorrow to **celebrate** properly.

As Jack wheels me back to Mum, we pass Mrs Taylor. She smiles at me, and right now in this moment, I know anything is **possible**.

Chapter 12

BESTIES

The next day is the first day of the school holidays. Flo pushes me to the shops to buy some **celebratory** lemonade. As we pass the charity shop, Annie waves at us, looking very pleased with herself. She is standing on the newly made ramp.

'We'll come and visit soon,'

shouts Flo from across the road, and Annie gives us a thumbs up.

When we get home, Liv has arrived to celebrate our **VICTORY**. This time, there is no flood. She has brought funny-looking **cakes** with her. She says they are **lamingtons**. They are cake squares rolled in chocolate icing and covered in coconut. They look **delicious**. Liv says today is National Lamington Day in Australia. Everyone in Australia eats lamingtons on this day.

We sit around the kitchen table, me, Miya, Jack, Flo and Liv, and celebrate our win with an Australian lamington.

Jack already has chocolate smeared around his face.

Liv shows us photos of her parents on a beach in Bondi, which is in Australia. They are smiling and wearing sunglasses, with sand and sea stretching for miles behind them. Liv is so **excited** because her mum and dad fly into London tomorrow. It has been four weeks since she has seen them.

She seems much **happier** and says she doesn't want to leave our school. She says she would miss her new **BEST FRIENDS** too much!

Liv says one day maybe we could all go for a visit to Australia. We agree that this is a brilliant idea. A trip to Australia with our **new friend**, Liv.

ALEX FIELD

Alex Field has written twelve books. *I'm a Tiger* was shortlisted for the Speech Pathology Australia Book of the Year Award. Alex's son used a communication aid much like the one Ava uses to speak. Alex and her son had lots of conversations about really important things like cricket and food, especially cake. Alex has spent half her life living in Sydney, Australia and the other half living in London, England. She wishes there was a plane that could take her from London to Sydney in two hours instead of 21 hours!

Joanna Bartel

Joanna Bartel is an Australian illustrator with a background in graphic design and secondary school art/design and English teaching. She draws much of her inspiration from everyday family life with three young kids, experiences in teaching, and childhood memories of fun with three brothers and lots of cousins. Joanna has a particular love for character design and celebrating diversity.